CU00688214

Wise Men Talking Series

MENCIUS
孟子说 Says

蔡希勤 编注

□ 责任编辑 **韩晖**

□ 翻译 **何祚康 郁苓**

□ 绘图 **李士伋**

老人家说系列丛书

华语教学出版社
SINOLINGUA

First Edition 2006

Second Printing 2007

Third Printing 2009

ISBN 978-7-80200-212-8

Copyright 2006 by Sinolingua

Published by Sinolingua

24 Baiwanzhuang Road, Beijing 100037, China

Tel: (86) 10-68320585

Fax: (86) 10-68326333

http://www.sinolingua.com.cn

E-mail: hyjx@sinolingua.com.cn

Printed by Beijing Foreign Languages Printing House

Distributed by China International Book Trading Corporation

35 Chegongzhuang Xilu, P. O. Box 399

Beijing 100044, China

Printed in the People's Republic of China

老人家说
Wise Men Talking

俗曰:"不听老人言,吃亏在眼前。"

老人家走的路多,吃的饭多,看的书多,经的事多,享的福多,受的罪多,可谓见多识广,有丰富的生活经验,老人家说的话多是经验之谈,后生小子不可不听也。

在中国历史上,春秋战国时期是中国古代思想高度发展的时期,那个时候诸子并起,百家争鸣,出现了很多"子"字辈的老人家,他们有道家、儒家、墨家、名家、法家、兵家、阴阳家,多不胜数,车载斗量,一时星河灿烂。

后来各家各派的代表曾先后聚集于齐国稷下学宫,齐宣王是个开明的诸侯王,因纳无盐丑女钟离春为后而名声大噪,对各国来讲学的专家学者不问来路一律管吃管住,享受政府津贴,对愿留下来做官的,授之以客卿,造巨室,付万钟。对不愿做官的,也给予"不治事而议论"之特殊待遇。果然这些人各为其主,各为其派,百家争鸣,百花齐放,设坛辩论,著书立说:有的说仁,有的说义,有的说无为,有的说逍遥,有的说非攻,有的说谋攻,有的说性善,有的说性恶,有的说亲非亲,有的说马非马,知彼知己,仁者无敌……留下了很多光辉灿烂的学术经典。

可惜好景不长,秦始皇时丞相李斯递话说"焚书坑儒",结果除秦记、医药、卜筮、种树书外,民间所藏诗、书及百家典籍一把火烧个精光。到西汉武帝时,董仲舒又上了个折子,提出"罢黜百家,独尊儒术",从此,儒学成了正统,"黄老、刑名百家之言"成为邪说。

"有德者必有言",儒学以外的各家各派虽屡被扫荡,却不断变幻着生存方式以求不灭,并为我们保存下了十分丰富的经典著作。在这些经典里,先哲们留下了很多充满智慧和哲理的、至今仍然熠熠发光的至理名言,我们将这些各家各派的老人家的"金玉良言"编辑成这套《老人家说》丛书,加以注释并译成英文,采取汉英对照出版,以飨海内外有心有意于中国传统文化的广大读者。

As the saying goes, "If an old dog barks, he gives counsel."

Old men, who walk more roads, eat more rice, read more books, have more experiences, enjoy more happiness, and endure more sufferings, are experienced and knowledgeable, with rich life experience. Thus, what they say is mostly wise counsel, and young people should listen to them.

The Spring and Autumn (722 – 481 BC) and War-ring States (475 – 221 BC) periods of Chinese history were a golden age for ancient Chinese thought. In those periods, various schools of thought, together with many sages whose names bore the honorific suffix " Zi ", e-merged and contended, including the Taoist school, Confucian school, Mohist school, school of Logicians, Legalist school, Military school and Yin-Yang school. Numerous and well known, these schools of thought were as brilliant as the Milky Way.

Later representatives of these schools of thought flocked to the Jixia Academy of the State of Qi. Duke Xuan of Qi was an enlightened ruler, famous for making an ugly but brilliant woman his empress. The duke pro-vided board and lodging, as well as government subsi-dies for experts and scholars coming to give lectures, and never inquired about their backgrounds. For those willing to hold official positions, the duke appointed them guest officials, built mansions for them and paid them high salaries. Those unwilling to take up official posts were kept on as advisors. This was an era when "one hundred schools of thought contended and a hundred flowers blossomed." The scholars debated in forums, and wrote books to expound their doctrines: Some preached benevolence; some, righteousness; some, inaction; some, absolute freedom; some, aversion to offensive war; some, attack by stratagem; some, the goodness of man's nature; some, the evil nature of man. Some said that relatives were not relatives; some said that horses were not horses; some urged the importance of knowing oneself and one's enemy; some said that benevolence knew no enemy... And they left behind many splendid classic works of scholarship.

Unfortunately, this situation did not last long. When Qin Shihuang (reigned 221 – 206 BC) united all the states of China, and ruled as the First Emperor, his prime minister, Li Si, ordered that all books except those on medicine, fortune telling and tree planting be burned. So, all poetry collections and the classics of the various schools of thought were destroyed. Emperor Wu (reigned 140 – 88 BC) of the Western Han Dynasty made Confucianism the orthodox doctrine of the state, while other schools of thought, including the Taoist and Legalist schools, were deemed heretical.

These other schools, however, managed to survive, and an abundance of their classical works have been handed down to us. These classical works contain many wise sayings and profound insights into philosophical theory which are still worthy of study today. We have compiled these nuggets of wisdom uttered by old men of the various ancient schools of thought into this series Wise Men Talking, and added explanatory notes and English translation for the benefit of both Chinese and overseas readers fond of traditional Chinese culture.

IV

目录

CONTENTS

1

不挟长，不挟贵〔10〕

The principle（of friendship）is not to take advantage of one's seniority or high position or the high positions of one's relatives.

不信仁贤，则国空虚〔12〕

If virtuous and talented men are not trusted, then the state will be devoid of all good men.

C

恻隐之心，人皆有之〔14〕

Compassion is common to all...

恻隐之心，仁之端也〔16〕

A sense of sympathy is the beginning of being benevolent.

春秋无义战〔18〕

There were no just wars in the Spring and Autumn Period.

D

得道者多助，失道者寡助〔20〕

Practicing a policy of benevolence wins support from the people; otherwise the support of the people will be lost.

得志，与民由之〔22〕

When a gentleman is in power, he should follow the

right course together with the people.

道在迩而求诸远〔24〕

One walks from the near to the distant and starts with the
easy and moves on to the difficult.

F

反身而诚，乐莫大焉〔26〕

There can be no greater pleasure than to find, after
reflection, oneself sincere.

非其道，则一箪食不可受于人〔28〕

I would not accept even one meal if it was not taken in
accordancne with the right way.

富贵不能淫，贫贱不能移〔30〕

Wealth and power cannot corrupt him, poverty can not
sway his principles...

G

恭者不侮人，俭者不夺人〔32〕

A courteous man will not insult others; a self-restrained
man will not rob others.

古之君子，过则改之〔34〕

A benevolent ruler in ancient times would correct his

mistakes.

古之君子，其过也，如日月之食〔36〕

The mistakes of ancient rulers were like solar and lunar

eclipese...

规矩，方员之至也〔38〕

The compass and the T-square are the criteria of circles

and squares.

J

桀纣之失天下也，失其民也〔40〕

The reason Jie and Zhou failed to keep their empires is

that they had lost the support and confidence of their people.

今夫弈之为数，小数也〔42〕

Though chess-playing is a petty skill...

尽信书，则不如无书〔44〕

To believe unconditionally what the *Book of History* says

is worse than if there were no *Book of History* in existence.

居天下之广居〔46〕

(As for males) the guiding principle should be benevolence.

君仁，莫不仁〔48〕

If rulers are benevolent, then all their people will be

benevolent too.

君子莫大乎与人为善〔50〕

The best virtue of a gentleman is to do good things for
the benefit of others.

君子引而不发，跃如也〔52〕

A gentleman trains others in the way Yi taught archery...

K

孔子登东山而小鲁〔54〕

When Confucius ascended the Eastern Mountain, he
realized how small the State of Lu was.

L

老吾老，以及人之老〔56〕

Extend your respect for your aged parents to all the aged.

乐民之乐者〔58〕

If a king takes his people's delights as his own delights...

离娄之明〔60〕

Even with Li Lou's eyesight...

令闻广誉施于身〔62〕

When one enjoys a good reputation in society...

M

民为贵〔64〕

To a state, the people are the most important thing.

民之归仁也，犹水之就下〔66〕

People will submit to policies of benevolence as water
flows downhill. . .

明君制民之产〔68〕

A wise king would see to it that his people have enough
wherewith. . .

Q

亲亲，仁也〔70〕

To love one's parents is benevolence. . .

穷则独善其身〔72〕

In obscurity, scholars would maintain their own integrity.

权，然后知轻重〔74〕

One knows the weight after weighing it. . .

R

人必自侮，然后人侮之〔76〕

A person can only be insulted when his own behavior
invites insults.

人不可以无耻〔78〕

Men should not be without a sense of shame.

人皆有不忍人之心〔80〕

Everyone has a heart of mercy.

人皆有所不忍〔82〕

Everyone has something that he cannot bear.

人人亲其亲，长其长〔84〕

If one loves his parents and respects his seniors, the world will be at peace.

人有不为也，而后可以有为〔86〕

A person can make some achievement only when there is something that he does not do.

人之患在好为人师〔88〕

The trouble with people is that they are too eager to assume the role of teacher.

人之所不学而能者，其良能也〔90〕

What men can do without learning is a result of inborn ability.

人之有道也，饱食、煖衣〔92〕

Human beings would not be far from animals and birds if they had only enough food to eat...

仁，人之安宅也〔94〕

Benevolence is where one should reside. . .

仁也者，人也〔96〕

To be benevolent is to be human.

仁言不如仁声之入人深也〔98〕

Benevolent words do not strike root in the heart of people as much as benevolent music does.

仁则荣，不仁则辱〔100〕

Practicing a policy of benevolence leads to glory; otherwise humiliation occurs.

仁者爱人〔102〕

A benevolent person loves others. . .

仁者如射〔104〕

A benevolent man should be like an archer. . .

仁者无敌〔106〕

He who practices benevolence is invincible!

仁之胜不仁也，犹水胜火〔108〕

Benevolence can overcome cruelty, as water can extinguish fire.

入则无法家拂士〔110〕

A state has no chance of surviving if there are no strict,
law-enforcing ministers...

S

上无道揆也，下无法守也〔112〕

If the ones high up hold no moral principles, then there

will be no law for the ones low down.

上有好者，下必有甚焉者矣〔114〕

Inferiors are keen to do more of what their superiors are

fond of doing.

生亦我所欲，所欲有甚于生者〔116〕

Though life is what I treasure, there is something that is

more precious to me...

声闻过情，君子耻之〔118〕

A gentleman is ashamed of his reputation surpassing his

qualities.

士穷不失义〔120〕

Scholars will not drop righteousness in adversity...

顺天者存，逆天者亡〔122〕

Those who follow Heaven's will survive and those who

disobey Heaven's will perish.

虽有天下易生之物也〔124〕

Even a plant that grows readily will not be able to grow...

T

天将降大任于是人也〔126〕

When Heaven intends to bestow a great mission on a person...

天时不如地利〔128〕

Favorable weather is less important than advantageous terrain.

天下不心服而王者，未之有也〔130〕

One can never unify the world if the hearts of all the people are not won over.

天下溺，援之以道〔132〕

If all the people of the world are drowning, they are to be saved by means of the Way.

天下有道，小德役大德〔134〕

When the world is in good order, people of low morality listen to people of high morality...

天下有道，以道殉身〔136〕

When the rule of the empire is in order, a gentleman immerses himself in principles.

天下之本在国〔138〕

Kingdoms are the basis of the empire...

天下之言性也，则故而已矣〔140〕

When one talks about the nature of something, he needs

to know how it comes to be what it is...

W

为高必因丘陵〔142〕

Lofty platforms should be built on mountains.

我善养吾浩然之气〔144〕

I am good at cultivating the great moral force.

无恒产而有恒心者〔146〕

Only scholars can be morally confident though they possess

no property.

无为其所不为〔148〕

Do not do what you should not do...

X

西子蒙不洁，则人皆掩鼻而过之〔150〕

If Xi Zi were covered in filth, everyone would pass her

by holding his nose.

贤者以其昭昭使人昭昭〔152〕

Virtuous men, in instructing others, get themselves

enlightened first. . .

贤者在位，能者在职〔154〕

Employ virtuous persons as officials and assign capable

persons to important posts.

小固不可以敌大〔156〕

It seems that a small kingdom cannot defeat a big kingdom.

形色，天性也〔158〕

Bodily form and appearance are endowed by Heaven. . .

Y

言近而指远者，善言也〔160〕

Simple words with far-reaching meaning are good words.

言人之不善〔162〕

What shall a man do when he meets with some misfor-

tune. . .

言无实不祥〔164〕

It is not right to utter empty words. . .

养心莫善于寡欲〔166〕

The best way to cultivate one's heart is to reduce one's

desires.

仰不愧于天〔168〕

The second delight of a gentleman is that he feels no shame as he faces Heaven above...

尧舜之道〔170〕

Even with Yao and Shun's statecraft...

一正君而国定矣〔172〕

When rulers' errors are corrected their kingdoms will be stable.

以力服人者，非心服也〔174〕

When one dominates others by force, they do not submit to him sincerely...

以佚道使民，虽劳不怨〔176〕

If people are employed in order to ease their lot, they will not begrudge it even if they are driven hard.

友也者，友其德也〔178〕

When one befriends others, what he should take into consideration is the others' good qualities and not other things.

有不虞之誉〔180〕

There is unexpected praise and highly demanding censure.

有恒产者有恒心〔182〕

People observe moral concepts and codes of behavior

only when they have regular incomes from their property.

有为者辟若掘井〔184〕

Trying to achieve something is like digging a well. . .

鱼，我所欲也〔186〕

Fish is what I want. . .

域民不以封疆之界〔188〕

National border alone can not stop people from fleeing.

欲贵者，人之同心也〔190〕

Everyone shares the aspiration for honor.

Z

执中无权，犹执一也〔192〕

To adhere to the middle way without being flexible is being

stubbornly biased.

志士不忘在沟壑〔194〕

A person with lofty ideals would not hesitate to have

his corpse abandoned in the wilderness.

中也养不中〔196〕

Men of lofty morality should educate and influence men

of doubtful morality.

诸侯之宝三〔198〕

For the lords of the states there are three treasures.

尊贤使能〔200〕

A king should respect virtuous persons, employ capable

persons. . .

孟子说

MENCIUS SAYS

　　孟子,姓孟名轲,字子舆。战国邹国人。春秋鲁公族孟氏之后。公元前390年(周安王十二年)秋八月孟子父母朝峄山,在回来的路上孟子出生,因生在马车上故取名轲字子舆。

　　孟子自称为孔子"私淑弟子","受业于子思之门人"。曾至齐稷下,一度任齐宣王客卿,中年以后游历各国,晚年授徒讲学著书立说。一生推崇、学习孔子,提出以心释"仁",以义行"仁"的原则,被后世儒家尊为"亚圣",儒家学说也被称为"孔孟之道"。

　　孟子重义,其名言曰:"仁,人心也;义,人路也。""士穷不失义,达不离道。""人皆有所不忍,达之于其所忍,仁也;人皆有所不为,达之于其所为,义也。"

Mencius' name was Meng Ke with the courtesy name Ziyu. As a native of the State of Zou in the Warring States Period, he was descendant of the Meng clan of the State of Lu in the Warring States Period. In August 390 BC (the 12th year of King Anwang of Zhou) his parents went to Mount Yi. On the way back, Mencius was born in a cart, thus he was given the name Ke [meaning a cart in Chinese] and the courtesy name Ziyu.

Mencius called himself "a self-styled disciple" of Confucius, and "was taught by a disciple of Zisi" [who was generally identified as the grandson of Confucius]. He once went to the Jixia Academy of the State of Qi, and was a minister for King Xuanwang for a period. In his middle age, he started to travel around different states, and in his old days he taught students, gave lectures, and wrote books on his doctrines. Throughout his life, Mencius held Confucius in esteem and followed Confucius' doctrines. He put forward the principle to interpret "benevolence" with heart, and practice "benevolence" with righteousness, and thus was regarded with respect as "sub-sage" by subsequent Chinese philosophers, and Confucianism was called "doctrines of Confucius and Mencius."

Mencius laid stress on righteousness. His well-known sayings include: "Benevolence is man's heart; righteousness is man's way." "An intellectual does not relinquish righteousness even in poverty. Nor does he stray from the correct way in prosperity." "For everyone there are things that he cannot bear to see or to do. To have that sentiment also in what he can bring himself to do is benevolence. For everyone there are things that he is not willing to do. To apply that attitude also to what he does is righteousness."

爱人不亲，反其仁

When one loves but fails to receive love in return. . .

孟子说

爱人不亲,反其仁;治人不治,反其智;礼人不答,反其敬——行有不得者皆反求诸己,其身正而天下归之。

《孟子·离娄上》

When one loves but fails to receive love in return, one should reflect on whether one is really a benevolent man. When one fails to subject others to discipline, one should reflect on whether one knows the proper way to govern. When one fails to gain respect from others while treating others with the proper courtesies, one should reflect on whether one is sincere enough. One should reflect on oneself whenever one fails to get the expected results. If a ruler behaves correctly, all the people will pay allegiance to him.

【注释】

反其仁、反其智、反其敬:反问自身的意思。**反求诸己**:参见孔子的"反求诸其身"。(《礼记·中庸》)

【译文】

孟子说:"爱别人,却得不到别人的爱,就要反问自己是否真正有仁爱之心。管理别人,却没有管理好,就要反省自己的管理方法是否正确,知识是否够用。以礼待人却得不到别人的尊重,就要反责自己对别人的态度是否真诚。任何行为如果没有得到预期的效果都要反躬自责,自己的确端正了,天下人便会归向他。"

保民而王，莫之能御也

No man can be prevented from unifying the world if he unifies it by making the lives of the people stable.

保民而王，莫之能御也。

《孟子·梁惠王上》

No man can be prevented from unifying the world if he unifies it by making the lives of the people stable.

【注释】

保民而王，莫之能御也：齐宣王问孟子："您可以给我讲讲齐桓公、晋文公称霸诸侯的事吗？"孟子回答说："孔子的学生们没有谈到过齐桓公、晋文公的事，所以没有传下来，我也不曾听说过。您如果一定让我说，我就说说用道德的力量统一天下的'王道'吧！"齐宣王问："要有什么样的道德才能统一天下呢？"孟子说了上面的话。

【译文】

孟子说："如果为着百姓们的生活安定而去统一天下，是没有人能够阻挡得了的。"

博學而詳說之

Learn extensively, expound in detail...

博学而详说之，将以反说约也。

《孟子·离娄下》

Learn extensively, expound in detail and explain the cardinal principles briefly on the basis of mastery of knowledge.

【注释】

反：回到，反回来。约：简略，简约。孟子这里说的是做学问由简到繁，再由繁到简的过程。

【译文】

孟子说："广博地学习，详细地解说，在融会贯通的基础上再简略地述说大义。"

不耻不若人，何若人有

If one does not feel ashamed to fall behind others, how can he ever catch up with them?

不以落后为耻，怎么能赶上别人呢？

不耻不若人，何若人有？

《孟子·尽心上》

If one does not feel ashamed to fall behind others, how can he ever catch up with them?

【注释】

耻：羞耻。是孔子伦理思想的概念之一。指一种道德的羞耻感。孔子提出"行己有耻。"（《论语·子路》）作为士的行为准则。他说"知耻近乎勇。"（《礼记·中庸》）孟子认为羞耻心对于人关系重大。他说："人不可以不知耻，无耻之耻无耻矣。"（《孟子·尽心上》）这种思想成为注重民族大义的知识分子的传统精神。

【译文】

孟子说："不以落后为耻，怎么能赶上别人呢？"

不挟长，不挟贵

The principle（of friendship）is not to take advantage of one's seniority or high position or the high positions of one's relatives.

不挟长，不挟贵，不挟兄弟而友。

《孟子·万章下》

The principle（of friendship）is not to take advantage of one's seniority or high position or the high positions of one's relatives.

【注释】

挟（xié）：倚仗，恃以自重。"不挟长，不挟贵，不挟兄弟"是孟子教导弟子交友的原则。他认为："交朋友，是看中朋友的品德而交，心中就不存在有任何倚仗的观念。"（《孟子·万章下》）

【译文】

孟子说："交朋友不倚仗自己年纪大，不倚仗自己地位高，不倚仗自己兄弟的富贵。"

不信仁贤，则国空虚

If virtuous and talented men are not trusted, then the state will be devoid of all good men.

不信仁贤，则国空虚；无礼义，
则上下乱；无政事，则财用不足。

《孟子·尽心下》

If virtuous and talented men are not trusted, then the state will be devoid of all good men. If the rites are not observed, then the relations between superior and inferior will be in confusion. If a government is not properly administered, then the state's resources will fail.

【注释】

空虚：没有人才。孟子的意思是如果执政者不能重视人才，那么有才能的人就会流失。上下：上下级官吏。政事：政治。

【译文】

孟子说："不信任仁德贤能的人，国家就会无人才选用；没有礼仪，上下级的关系就会混乱；没有好的政治，国家财政就会困难。"

恻隐之心，人皆有之

Compassion is common to all...

恻隐之心，人皆有之；羞恶之心，人皆有之；恭敬之心，人皆有之；是非之心，人皆有之。

《孟子·告子上》

Compassion is common to all; so are the senses of shame, respect, and right and wrong.

【注释】

恻隐之心：孟子指一种天赋的同情心，他还认为同情心是"仁"的萌芽。羞恶之心：孟子指一种天赋的羞耻心，又认为羞恶心是"义"的萌芽。恭敬之心：孟子指一种天赋的谦让心，又称"辞让之心"。又认为辞让心是"礼"的萌芽。是非之心：孟子指一种天赋的分辨是非之心，这种天生分辨是非的能力是"智"的萌芽。

【译文】

孟子说："同情心，每个人都有；羞耻心，每个人都有；恭敬心，每个人都有；是非心，每个人都有。"

惻隱之心，仁之端也

A sense of sympathy is the beginning of being benevolent.

恻隐之心，仁之端也；羞恶之心，义之端也；辞让之心，礼之端也；是非之心，智之端也。人之有是四端也，犹其有四体也。

《孟子·公孙丑上》

A sense of sympathy is the beginning of being benevolent; a sense of shame is the beginning of being just; a sense of modesty is the beginning of being polite; and a sense of right and wrong is the beginning of being wise. Men are born with these four senses, as with their four limbs.

【注释】

端：开头。四体：四肢。

【译文】

孟子说："同情心是仁的萌芽，羞耻心是义的萌芽，谦让之心是礼的萌芽，是非之心是智的萌芽。人有这四种心和有四肢一样是与生俱来的。"

春秋无义战

There were no just wars in the Spring and Autumn Period.

春秋无义战。彼善于此，则有之矣。征者，上伐下也，敌国不相征也。

《孟子·尽心下》

There were no just wars in the Spring and Autumn Period. Only some kings were better than others, and senior states could send punitive expeditions against states of lower status, but states of the same status could not send punitive expeditions against one another.

【注释】

春秋：时代名。上伐下：孔子说："天下有道，则礼乐征伐自天子出；天下无道，则礼乐征伐自诸侯出。"敌国：同等级的国家。

【译文】

孟子说："春秋时代没有正义战争。有的君主比别的国家的君主好一些是有的。但征伐，只能是上级讨伐下级，同等级的国家是不能互相征伐的。所以说春秋无义战。"

得道者多助，失道者寡助

Practicing a policy of benevolence wins support from the people ; otherwise the support of the people will be lost.

得道者多助，失道者寡助。寡助之至，亲戚畔之；多助之至，天下顺之。

《孟子·公孙丑下》

Practicing a policy of benevolence wins support from the people; otherwise the support of the people will be lost. If one loses the support of the people, even one's relatives will turn against one; if one wins the support of the people, all the people in the world will come to pledge allegiance

【注释】

得道：得治国之道，即指行仁政。亲戚：古代对亲戚有多种解释，孟子所指父母兄弟姐妹而已。畔：同"叛"。

【译文】

孟子说："行仁政就得人心，不行仁政便失人心。失人心的结果，连亲戚都会背叛他；得人心的结果，天下的人都会归顺他。"

得志，与民由之

When a gentleman is in power, he should follow the right course together with the people.

得志，与民由之；不得志，独行其道。

《孟子·滕文公下》

When a gentleman is in power, he should follow the right course together with the people; when he is not in power, he should still stick to his principles.

【注释】

由：走，经历。孟子还说过："穷则独善其身，达则兼善天下。"（《孟子．尽心上》）与此义同。

【译文】

孟子说："得志时，和百姓一起走正道；不得志的时候，也能独自坚持正确的原则。"

道在迩而求诸远

One walks from the near to the distant and starts with the easy and moves on to the difficult.

道在迩而求诸远，事在易而求诸难。

《孟子·离娄上》

One walks from the near to the distant and starts with the easy and moves on to the difficult.

【注释】

迩（ěr）：近。《诗经·周南·汝坟》："虽则如毁，父母孔迩。"注："迩，近也。"

【译文】

孟子说："走路由近及远，做事由易及难。"

反身而诚，乐莫大焉

There can be no greater pleasure than to find，after re-flection，oneself sincere.

反身而诚，乐莫大焉。强恕而行，求仁莫近焉。

《孟子·尽心上》

There can be no greater pleasure than to find, after reflection, oneself sincere. Persisting in treating others in the way one wishes to be treated is the shortest way to benevolence.

【注释】

反身：儒家一种修养方法，指通过反省来检验自己的思想和行为是否符合道德标准，即"反求诸其身"（《礼记·中庸》）。恕：孔子的伦理范畴之一，有推己及人，即希望人以对己的态度来对待别人之意。孔子说："其恕乎，己所不欲，勿施于人。"（《论语·卫灵公》）近：近路，捷径。

【译文】

孟子说："反躬自问，自己是真诚的，便是最大的快乐。坚持推己及人的恕道，这是达到仁德的捷径。"

非其道，则一箪食不可受于人

I would not accept even one meal if it was not taken in accordancne with the right way.

如果不合礼，连一顿饭也不可以接受。

非其道，则一箪食不可受于人；如其道，则舜受尧之天下，不以为泰。

《孟子·滕文公下》

I would not accept even one meal if it was not taken in accordancne with the right way. It was not excessive for Shun to take over the empire from Yao because it was taken according to the right way.

【注释】

箪（dān）：盛饭的竹器。**舜受尧之天下**：尧和舜，传为上古帝王。舜名重华，号有虞氏，史称虞舜。生于妫汭（今山西永济），年二十以孝闻名。在尧晚年因四岳举荐，代尧摄政。尧死后登帝位。**泰**：过甚。

【译文】

孟子说："如果不合礼，连一顿饭也不可以接受。如果合礼，像舜接受了尧的天下，也不以为过。"

富贵不能淫，贫贱不能移

Wealth and power cannot corrupt him，poverty can not sway his principles...

富贵不能淫，贫贱不能移，威武不能屈，此之谓大丈夫。

《孟子·滕文公下》

Wealth and power cannot corrupt him, poverty can not sway his principles and threats cannot make him bend. Only such a person can be called a gentleman.

【注释】

淫：惑乱。**移**：摇动。《孔·玉藻》："疾趋则欲发，而手足毋移。"**屈**：屈服，摧折。

【译文】

孟子说："富贵不能乱其心，贫贱不能变其志，威武不能屈其节，这才是大丈夫。"

恭者不侮人，俭者不夺人

A courteous man will not insult others; a self-restrained man will not rob others.

恭者不侮人，俭者不夺人。

《孟子·离娄上》

A courteous man will not insult others; a self-restrained man will not rob others.

【注释】

恭：有礼貌。《礼·曲礼上》："是以君子恭敬撙节。"疏："在貌为恭，在心为敬。"侮（wǔ）：欺负，凌辱。夺（duó）：强取。

【译文】

孟子说："有礼貌的人不会侮辱别人，节俭的人不会掠夺别人。"

古之君子，过则改之

A benevolent ruler in ancient times would correct his mistakes.

古之君子，过则改之；今之君子，过则顺之。

《孟子·公孙丑下》

A benevolent ruler in ancient times would correct his mistakes. But a ruler now would leave the mistake uncorrected and muddle through.

【注释】

君子：在儒家学说中，君子有多种含义，此指"在位者"。顺：顺着。《墨子·鲁问》："楚人顺流而进，迎流而退。"

【译文】

孟子说："古代有仁德的执政者，有错即改；今天的执政者，有了过错，竟将错就错。"

古之君子，其过也，如日月之食

The mistakes of ancient rulers were like solar and lunar eclipese...

古之君子，其过也，如日月之食，民皆见之；及其更也，民皆仰之。今之君子，岂徒顺之，又从为之辞。

《孟子·公孙丑下》

The mistakes of ancient rulers were like solar and lunar eclipese—they were known to all people. After they correcte their mistakes, people admired them all the more. But a ruler now would not only leave the mistakes uncorrected, he would make excuses for them.

【注释】

食：蚀。**仰之**：仰，指抬头看。此指日蚀月蚀复明而言，臣民对执政者改正错误，正如盼望日月复明一样，故说"仰之"。

【译文】

孟子说："古代的执政者，他的过错像日蚀月蚀一般挂在天上，老百姓都看得见。当他们改正以后，老百姓更加敬仰他们。今天的执政者，不仅将错就错，还一定要编造一番假道理来为错误辩护。"

规矩，方员之至也

The compass and the T-square are the criteria of circles and squares.

规矩，方员之至也；圣人，人伦之至也。

《孟子·离娄上》

The compass and the T-square are the criteria of circles and squares. Sages are the criterion of human relationships.

【注释】

规矩：校正圆形、方形的器具。员：同"圆"。至：极。人伦：阶级社会里人的等级关系。"使契为司徒，教以人伦；父子有亲，君臣有义，夫妇有别，长幼有叙，朋友有信"。（《孟子·滕文公上》）

【译文】

孟子说："规矩是方圆的准则，圣人是做人的准则。"

桀紂之失天下也，失其民也

The reason Jie and Zhou failed to keep their empires is that they had lost the support and confidence of their people.

桀纣之失天下也，失其民也；失其民者，失其心也。

《孟子·离娄上》

The reason Jie and Zhou failed to keep their empires is that they had lost the support and confidence of their people.

【注释】

桀纣之失天下也：桀，夏朝最后一代王。嗜酒好声色，淫乐无度，滥杀谏臣，商汤趁机伐夏，夏亡。纣，商朝最后一代王。即位后重赋聚财，广建宫室，长夜饮乐，得妲己而唯言是从。重用谀臣，诛杀谏臣。后周武王会合各路诸侯伐纣，纣死商亡。

【译文】

孟子说："夏桀和商纣丧失天下的原因，是由于失去了百姓的支持，失去了民心。"

今夫弈之为数，小数也

Though chess-playing is a petty skill...

今夫弈之为数，小数也；不专心致志，则不得也。

《孟子·告子上》

Though chess-playing is a petty skill, if one cannot devote his heart to it, he will not be able to master the skill.

【注释】

弈：围棋。数：技巧。孟子还讲了这样一个故事："奕秋是全国的棋圣。假如让他同时教两个学生，一个人专心致志，认真领会老师的讲解。另一个人虽也在听讲，而脑子里却在想入非非，心不在焉。这样，虽然他和人家一道学习，成绩肯定不如人家。这是因为他不如人家聪明吗？显然不是的。"

【译文】

孟子说："譬如下围棋，这虽不过是小技艺而已，如果不能专心致志，也是学不好的。"

尽信书，则不如无书

To believe unconditionally what the *Book of History* says is worse than if there were no *Book of History* in existence.

尽信书，则不如无书。

《孟子·尽心下》

To believe unconditionally what the *Book of History* says is worse than if there were no *Book of History* in existence.

【注释】

尽信书：孟子所说的"书"指《尚书》，《武成》是书中一篇。在此篇中讲到周武王伐纣时有"血流漂杵"的记载，孟子很怀疑这记载的真实性。他认为以至仁伐至不仁，是不可能流那么多血的。

【译文】

孟子说："完全相信书，则不如没有书。"

居天下之广居

（As for males）the guiding principle should be benevolence.

居天下之广居，立天下之正位，
行天下之大道。

《孟子·滕文公下》

(As for males) the guiding principle should be benevolence. His performance should conform to the rites and his behavior should be righteous and just.

【注释】

广居：天下最宽广的居处——仁。正位：天下最正确的位置——礼。大道：天下最宽广的路——义。"

【译文】

孟子说："（至于男子）应居之以仁，立之以礼，行之以义。"

君仁，莫不仁

If rulers are benevolent, then all their people will be benevolent too.

君仁，莫不仁；君义，莫不义；君正，莫不正。

《孟子·离娄上》

　　If rulers are benevolent, then all their people will be benevolent too. If rulers are righteous, then all their people will be righteous also. If rulers are upright, all their people will be upright also.

【注释】

　　孟子发展了孔子的"仁"说，提出以心释"仁"，以义行"仁"的原则。说："仁，人心也；义，人路也。"

【译文】

　　孟子说："君主仁，没有人不仁。君主义，没有人不义。君主正，没有人不正。"

君子莫大乎与人为善

The best virtue of a gentleman is to do good things for the benefit of others.

君子莫大乎与人为善。

《孟子·公孙丑上》

The best virtue of a gentleman is to do good things for the benefit of others.

【注释】

与人为善：助人相与为善。与，跟。为，做。善，好事。"取诸人以为善，是与人为善者也。"（《孟子·公孙丑上》）孟子还说过："达则兼善天下。"意谓不仅自身为善，还要使别人也达到善的境界。

【译文】

孟子说："君子最高的德行就是与人为善。"

君子引而不发，跃如也

A gentleman trains others in the way Yi taught archery...

君子引而不发，跃如也。

《孟子·尽心上》

A gentleman trains others in the way Yi taught archery. He drew bows without discharging the arrow, just to show his eagerness to shoot.

【注释】

引而不发，跃如也：引，拉弓。发，射箭。拉满了弓，却不发箭，作出跃跃欲试的样子。成语"引而不发"源于此，后比喻作好准备，待机行事。也常用以比喻善于启发引导学生或善于控制自己。

【译文】

孟子说："君子育人就像教人射箭一样，拉满了弓，却不发箭，作出跃跃欲试的样子。"

孔子登东山而小鲁

When Confucius ascended the Eastern Mountain, he realized how small the State of Lu was.

孔子登东山而小鲁，登泰山而小天下，故观于海者难为水，游于圣人之门者难为言。

《孟子·尽心上》

When Confucius ascended the Eastern Mountain, he realized how small the State of Lu was. When he ascended Mount Tai, he saw how small the empire was. Anyone who has seen the sea will not be impressed by other waters. Anyone who has learned from a sage will not be attracted by other doctrines.

【注释】

东山：一说即蒙山，在今山东省蒙阴县南。

【译文】

孟子说："孔子登上东山往下看，便觉得鲁国小了。登上泰山，便觉得天下也小了。所以对见过大海的人，别的水就难于吸引他了；对于曾在圣人之门学习过的人，别的学说也就难于吸引他了。"

老吾老，以及人之老

Extend your respect for your aged parents to all the aged.

老吾老，以及人之老；幼吾幼，以及人之幼。

《孟子·梁惠王上》

Extend your respect for your aged parents to all the aged，and extend your love for your own children to all children.

【注释】

老吾老，以及人之老：前一"老"，敬老。尊敬自己家族的长辈，从而推广到尊敬别人家的长辈。现在的社会只提"尊老"而不提"孝亲"，现在很多年轻人不孝敬父母，甚至不赡养父母。一个连自己父母都不孝敬的人，会尊敬别人的老人吗？

【译文】

孟子说："由尊敬自己的老人，从而推广到尊敬所有的老人；爱护自己的儿女，从而推广到爱护所有人家的儿女。"

乐民之乐者

If a king takes his people's delights as his own delights. . .

乐民之乐者，民亦乐其乐；忧民之忧者，民亦忧其忧。乐以天下，忧以天下，然而不王者，未之有也。

《孟子·梁惠王下》

If a king takes his people's delights as his own delights, then his people will take his delights as their own; if a king takes his people's sorrows as his own sorrows, then his people will take his sorrows as their own. Any king who shares delights and sorrows with his people is sure to dominate the world.

【译文】

孟子对齐宣王说："如果国君以百姓的欢乐为自己的欢乐，百姓也会以国君的欢乐为自己的欢乐；国君以百姓的忧愁为自己的忧愁，百姓也会以国君的忧愁为自己的忧愁。和天下百姓同忧同乐的国君，就能使天下归服于他。"

离娄之明

Even with Li Lou's eyesight. . .

离娄之明、公输子之巧，不以规矩，不能成方圆；师旷之聪，不以六律，不能正五音。

《孟子·离娄上》

Even with Li Lou's eyesight and Gongshu Zi's skill, no one can draw a square and a circle without proper tools. Even with Shi Kuang's hearing, no one can check the five notes without the help of the six musical scales.

【注释】

离娄：相传为黄帝时人，目力极强，能于百步之外看清秋毫之末。**公输子：**名般（一作"班"）鲁国人，又称鲁班。为中国古代著名巧匠。**师旷：**中国古代有名的音乐家，晋平公时任太师（乐官之长）。**六律：**指阳律六。**五音：**中国音阶名，即宫、商、角、徵、羽。

【译文】

孟子说："即使有离娄的视力，公输般的技巧，如果不借助于必要的工具，也不能画出标准的方形和圆形。即便有师旷那样的审音听力，如果不借助于六律，也不能正确校正五音。"

令闻广誉施于身

When one enjoys a good reputation in society...

令闻广誉施于身，所以不愿人之文绣也。

《孟子·告子上》

When one enjoys a good reputation in society, one does not hanker after others' finery.

【注释】

令闻：好名声。文绣：古代必须有爵命的人才能着文绣之服。

【译文】

孟子说："自己身上有社会公认的美名，也就不会羡慕别人的锦衣绣服了。"

民为贵

To a state, the people are the most important thing.

民为贵，社稷次之，君为轻。

《孟子·尽心下》

To a state, the people are the most important thing, the altars to the gods of earth and grain come second, and the ruler is the least important thing.

【注释】

社稷：古代帝王、诸侯所祭的土神和谷神。人非土不立，非谷不食，故封土立社，示有土也；稷，五谷之长，故立稷而祭之。历代封建王朝必先立社稷坛。灭亡一个国家后，必先变置该国的社稷。因后多以社稷为国家政权的标志。**民贵君轻：**孟子的政治主张，体现了先秦儒家民本主义思想。

【译文】

孟子说："对一个国家来说，百姓最重要，社稷次之，君主为轻。"

民之归仁也，犹水之就下

People will submit to policies of benevolence as water flows downhill. . .

民之归仁也，犹水之就下、兽之走圹也。故为渊驱鱼者，獭也；为丛驱爵者，鹯也；为汤武驱民者，桀与纣也。

《孟子·离娄上》

People will submit to policies of benevolence as water flows downhill and animals gather in deserted land and forests. Just as the otter drives fish into deep ponds and the eagle drives birds into the forests, so Jie of the Xia Dynasty and Zhou of the Shang Dynasty drove the people into the arms of Tand of Shang Dynasty and King Wu of the Zhou Dynasty.

【注释】

獭（tǎ）：水獭。爵：同"雀"。鹯（zhān）：一种猛禽，一说鹞鹰。

【译文】

孟子说："百姓归附于仁政，好像水往低处流，野兽向旷野山林一样自然。所以，把鱼赶入深池的是水獭，把鸟雀赶入树林的是鹞鹰，把百姓赶到商汤、周武王一边的正是夏桀和商纣。"

明君制民之产

A wise king would see to it that his people have enough wherewith. . .

明君制民之产，必使仰足以事父母，俯足以畜妻子，乐岁终身饱，凶年免于死亡；然后驱而之善，故民之从之也轻。

《孟子·梁惠王上》

A wise king would see to it that his people have enough wherewith to support their parents and to feed their wives and children, that they have enough food and clothes in years of good harvests, and do not perish in years of bad harvests. Then the people would listen when taught, and follow what is right.

【注释】

乐岁：丰收之年。凶年：灾年。驱：驱使，逼迫。轻：轻易，容易。

【译文】

孟子说："贤明的君主要使老百姓的产业收入上可以赡养父母，下足以抚养妻子儿女；好年成可以丰衣足食，坏年成也不至于饿死。然后再给他们讲从善的道理，老百姓自然就容易接受。"

亲亲，仁也

To love one's parents is benevolence. . .

亲亲，仁也；敬长，义也；无他，达之天下也。

《孟子·尽心上》

To love one's parents is benevolence and to respect one's elder brother is righteousness. Only these two virtues, benevolence and righteousness, are universal virtues.

【注释】

仁、义：孟子提出"仁，人心也；义，人路也。"（《孟子·告子上》）这种以心释仁，以义行仁的原则确立了孟子在儒学传统中的地位。

【译文】

孟子说："爱亲为仁，敬长为义，只有仁和义是通达天下的两种品德。"

穷则独善其身

In obscurity, scholars would maintain their own integrity.

穷则独善其身，达则兼善天下。

《孟子·尽心上》

In obscurity, scholars would maintain their own integrity. In times of success, they would make perfect the whole empire.

【注释】

独善、兼善：独善，保持个人的节操。兼善，不仅求得自身的善，并且使别人也达到善的境界。

【译文】

孟子说："穷困时则独善其身，显贵时则兼善天下。"

权，然后知轻重

One knows the weight after weighing it...

孟子说

权，然后知轻重；度，然后知长短。物皆然，心为甚。

《孟子·梁惠王上》

One knows the weight after weighing it and one knows the distance after measuring it. This principle applies to all things, and especially to popular feelings.

【注释】

权：称锤，测定物体重量的器具，亦指称重量。度：计量长短的标准。

【译文】

孟子对齐宣王说："称一称，才知道轻重；量一量，才知道长短。什么东西都是这样，人心更是如此。"

人必自侮，然后人侮之

A person can only be insulted when his own behavior invites insults.

人必自侮，然后人侮之；家必自毁，而后人毁之；国必自伐，而后人伐之。

《孟子·离娄上》

A person can only be insulted when his own behavior invites insults; a family will be destroyed only when it has destroyed itself beforehand, and a kingdom will be invaded only when it provides a cause.

【注释】

家：指卿大夫的采地食邑。国：指诸侯国。

【译文】

孟子说："人必先有遭侮辱的行为，才会遭别人侮辱；家必先有被毁坏的因素，外力才能毁坏它；国必先有被讨伐的原因，才会被别国讨伐。"

人不可以无耻

Men should not be without a sense of shame.

人不可以无耻，无耻之耻，无耻矣。

《孟子·尽心上》

Men should not be without a sense of shame. Not knowing shame is indeed shameless.

【注释】

无耻：儒家强调知耻。《礼记·中庸》："知耻近乎勇。"孔子和孟子都重视教育学生知耻。孔子说"行己以耻。"（《论语·子路》）

【译文】

孟子说："人不可以没有羞耻之心，不知羞耻的那种羞耻，是真的不知羞耻。"

人皆有不忍人之心

Everyone has a heart of mercy.

人皆有不忍人之心。先王有不忍人之心，斯有不忍人之政矣。以不忍人之心，行不忍人之政，治天下可运之掌上。

《孟子·公孙丑上》

Everyone has a heart of mercy. Ancient kings were merciful so their governments were merciful. To practice forbearance with such a heart, running a state will be as easy as turning over one's hand.

【注释】

不忍人之心：怜悯别人之心。**先王：**先秦儒家对古代圣明君主的一种称呼。

【译文】

孟子说："每个人都有怜悯别人之心。先王因为有怜悯别人之心，则有怜悯别人的政治。以怜悯别人之心实施怜悯别人的政治，治理天下则易如反掌。"

人皆有所不忍

Everyone has something that he cannot bear.

老人家说系列丛书　孟子说

人皆有所不忍，达之于其所忍，仁也；人皆有所不为，达之于其所为，义也。

《孟子·尽心上》

Everyone has something that he cannot bear. To extend such aversion to what he can bear is benevolence. Everyone has something that he refuses to do. To extend such aversion to what he is willing to do is righteousness.

【注释】

不忍：不忍心干的事。达：扩充，扩大。不为：不忍为。

【译文】

孟子说："每个人都有不忍心干的事，把这种心情扩充到所忍心干的事上，便是仁。每个人都有不肯干的事，把它扩充到所肯干的事上，便是义。"

人人亲其亲，长其长

If one loves his parents and respects his seniors, the world will be at peace.

人人亲其亲，长其长，而天下平。

《孟子·离娄下》

If one loves his parents and respects his seniors, the world will be at peace.

【注释】

亲其亲、长其长：亲爱自己的亲人，恭敬自己的长辈。

【译文】

孟子说："只要人人能亲爱自己的双亲，尊敬自己的长辈，天下就会太平。"

人有不为也，而后可以有为

A person can make some achievement only when there is something that he does not do.

人要有所不为，才能有所为。

人有不为也，而后可以有为。

《孟子·离娄下》

A person can make some achievement only when there is something that he does not do.

【注释】

不为、有为：不作为；有所作为。

【译文】

孟子说："人要有所不为，才能有所为。"

人之患在好为人师

The trouble with people is that they are too eager to assume the role of teacher.

人之患在好为人师。

《孟子·离娄上》

The trouble with people is that they are too eager to assume the role of teacher.

【注释】

患（huàn）：忧虑，担心。**好为人师**：好（hào），喜欢，不谦虚，喜欢以教导者自居。

【译文】

孟子说："人最怕总喜欢做人家的老师。"

人之所不學而能者，其良能也

What men can do without learning is a result of inborn ability.

人之所不学而能者，其良能也；
所不虑而知者，其良知也。

《孟子·尽心上》

What men can do without learning is a result of inborn ability; what men know without contemplating is a result of intuition.

【注释】

良能：天赋最好的能力。不用学习而自然就能者，是谓良能也。也就是孔子说的"生而知之者"。（《论语·季氏》）良知：天赋的分辨是非善恶的智能。不待思虑而自然知者，是谓良知也。

【译文】

孟子说："人不待学习便能做到的，这是本能；不待思考便知道的，这是先知。"

人之有道也，飽食、煖衣

Human beings would not be far from animals and birds if they had only enough food to eat...

人之有道也，饱食、煖衣、逸居而无教，则近于禽兽。

《孟子·滕文公上》

Human beings would not be far from animals and birds if they had only enough food to eat, enough clothes to wear and enough shelter but no education.

【注释】

人之有道也：有，为也。有道，为道。煖（xuān）：温暖。

【译文】

孟子说："人之所以为人，只是吃饱穿暖，住得安逸了是远远不够的，如果没有教育，也就和禽兽没什么差别了。"

仁，人之安宅也

Benevolence is where one should reside. . .

仁，人之安宅也；义，人之正路
也。旷安宅而弗居，舍正路而不由，
哀哉！

《孟子·离娄上》

Benevolence is where one should reside; justice is the right road along which one should go. It is a pity to refuse to reside where one should reside and depart from the road one should follow!

【注释】

安宅：安居。孟子认为仁是人的安宅。正路：大路。

【译文】

孟子说："仁是人应居之处，义是人之正路。舍应居之处不居，舍正道不走，乃是人之悲哀。"

仁也者，人也

To be benevolent is to be human.

仁也者，人也。合而言之，道也。

《孟子·尽心下》

To be benevolent is to be human. The joining of the two means principles.

【注释】

仁者人也：古音"仁"与"人"相同。《说文》曰："仁，亲也。从人二。"意思是只要有两个人在一起，就不能不有仁的道德，而仁的道德也只能在人与人之间产生。《礼记·中庸》也有"仁者，人也"。

【译文】

孟子说："仁的意思就是人，仁和人合在一起说，就是道。"

仁言不如仁声之入人深也

Benevolent words do not strike root in the heart of people as much as benevolent music does.

仁言不如仁声之入人深也，善政不如善教之得民也。善政，民畏之；善教，民爱之。善政得民财，善教得民心。

《孟子·尽心上》

Benevolent words do not strike root in the heart of people as much as benevolent music does. Good government does not win the hearts of the people as much as good education does. People fear good government, but they love good education. Good government can obtain the wealth created by the people, but good education can win the hearts of the people.

【注释】

仁言：仁德的话。仁声：仁德的音乐。指古代乐曲《雅》、《颂》的演奏声。善政：良好的政治。善教：良好的教育。民财：老百姓创造的财富。

【译文】

孟子说："仁德的话不如仁德的音乐深入人心；良好的政治不如良好的教育容易获得民心。良好的政治，百姓畏惧它；良好的教育，百姓爱它。良好的政治能得到百姓创造的财富，良好的教育能得到百姓的心。"

仁则荣，不仁则辱

Practicing a policy of benevolence leads to glory; otherwise humiliation occurs.

仁则荣，不仁则辱；今恶辱而居不仁，是犹恶湿而居下也。

《孟子·公孙丑上》

Practicing a policy of benevolence leads to glory; otherwise humiliation occurs. Nowadays, although men in power detest humiliation, they do not practice a policy of benevolence. This is like detesting moisture but living in low-lying land.

【注释】

仁则荣，不仁则辱：指诸侯以及卿相而言，这两句省略了主语。居不仁：行为不仁。

【译文】

孟子说："如果实行仁政，就会得到荣耀；如果不行仁政，就会遭受屈辱。如今的执政者，都不想遭受屈辱但又不肯行仁政，这好比厌恶潮湿却又自居于低洼之地一样。"

仁者爱人

A benevolent person loves others. . .

仁者爱人，有礼者敬人。爱人者，人恒爱之；敬人者，人恒敬之。

《孟子·离娄下》

A benevolent person loves others and a polite man respects others. The ones who love others will always be loved by others and the one who respect others will always be respected by others.

【注释】

恒：长久，经常。

【译文】

孟子说："仁人爱人，有礼的人懂得恭敬别人。爱别人的人，别人也会爱他。懂得恭敬别人的人，别人也会恭敬他。"

仁者如射

A benevolent man should be like an archer...

仁者如射：射者正己而后发；发而不中，不怨胜己者，反求诸己而已矣。

《孟子·公孙丑上》

A benevolent man should be like an archer who takes part in a shooting match and adjusts his posture before shooting. If he misses the target, he should not blame the winners, but seek the cause in himself.

【注释】

射：射箭的知识技能，古代教育内容的六艺之一。西周时，天子即以试射的办法来选拔人才。以射中次数的多少作为录用的标准。射者的行动是否合于礼仪也是评定的标准。**反求诸己**：儒家一种重要的修养方法，通过反省检验自己的思想和行为是否符合道德标准。孔子说："射有似乎君子。失诸正鹄，反求诸其身。"（《礼记·中庸》）

【译文】

孟子说："有仁德的人好比参加射箭比赛的射手一样：先端正自己的姿势而后放箭，如果没有射中，也不要埋怨那些胜过自己的人，只在自己身上找原因就是了。"

仁者无敌

He who practices benevolence is invincible!

仁者无敌。

《孟子·梁惠王上》

He who practices benevolence is invincible!

【注释】

仁：古代一种含义广泛的道德观念，其核心指人与人相亲，爱人。孔子贵仁，他说："夫仁者，己欲立而立人，己欲达而达仁。"孟子发展了孔子的"仁"说，提出以心释"仁"，以义行"仁"的原则。他说："仁，人心也；义，人路也。"

【译文】

孟子对梁惠王说："执政者行仁政将无敌于天下。"

仁之胜不仁也，犹水胜火

Benevolence can overcome cruelty, as water can extinguish fire.

仁之胜不仁也，犹水胜火。

《孟子·告子上》

Benevolence can overcome cruelty, as water can extinguish fire.

【注释】

水胜火：水可以灭火。孟子说："今天所谓行仁的人，好像用一杯水来扑灭一车柴的大火，火不能灭，便说水不能灭火，也就不再相信仁胜过不仁的道理。于是这些人又和不仁的人走在了一起，结果连他们已行的一点仁也消失了。"（《孟子·告子上》）

【译文】

孟子说："仁胜过不仁，正像水可以灭火一样。"

入则无法家拂士

A state has no chance of surviving if there are no strict, law-enforcing ministers...

入则无法家拂士，出则无敌国外患者，国恒亡。然后知生于忧患而死于安乐也。

《孟子·告子下》

A state has no chance of surviving if there are no strict, law-enforcing ministers and scholars capable of offering good advice in court and no constant threats of foreign aggression to guard against. And so we can conclude from this that worry and trouble enable one to survive, while complacency and pleasure will bring about one's downfall.

【注释】

入：指国内。**法家**：指守法度的世臣。**拂士**：拂（bì），矫正，通"弼"。指能够直谏矫正君王过失的人。**出**：指国外。

【译文】

孟子说："一个国家，国内没有执法严厉的大臣和足以辅弼的士人，国外没有相与抗衡的邻国和外患的忧虑，反倒容易被灭亡。这样，就可以知道忧虑患难足以使人生存，安逸快乐足以使人灭亡的道理了。"

上无道揆也，下无法守也

If the ones high up hold no moral principles, then there will be no law for the ones low down.

上无道揆也，下无法守也，朝不信道，工不信度，君子犯义，小人犯刑，国之所存者幸也。

《孟子·离娄上》

If the ones high up hold no moral principles, then there will be no law for the ones low down. If the court does not believe in morality and justice, craftsmen will disregard the rules. If officials break the laws, then ordinary people will do the same. In this way, the state will be in danger.

【注释】

上无道揆也：道揆，以义理度量事物。下无法守也：法守，按法度履行自己的职守。朝：朝廷。工：工匠。

【译文】

孟子说"在上的没有道德规范，在下的就无法可依，朝廷不相信道义，工匠不相信尺度，官吏破坏法度，百姓就会触犯刑法，这样的国家就很危险了。"

上有好者，下必有甚焉者矣

Inferiors are keen to do more of what their superiors are fond of doing.

老人家说系列丛书 孟子说

上有好者，下必有甚焉者矣。君子之德，风也；小人之德，草也。草尚之风，必偃。

《孟子·滕文公上》

Inferiors are keen to do more of what their superiors are fond of doing. Gentlemen are like the wind and petty persons are like grass, which bends with the wind.

【注释】

尚：同上。古"上"与"尚"常通用。偃（yǎn）：卧倒，倒伏。

【译文】

孟子说："在上位的人有什么爱好，下边的人一定爱得更加过分。君子好比风，小人好比草，风向哪边刮，草向哪边倒。"

生亦我所欲，所欲有甚于生者

Though life is what I treasure, there is something that is more precious to me...

生亦我所欲，所欲有甚于生者，故不为苟得也；死亦我所恶，所恶有甚于死者，故患有所不辟也。

《孟子·告子上》

Though life is what I treasure, there is something that is more precious to me, and that is righteousness. So I will not draw on an ignoble existence. Death is what I detest, but there is something that I detest more than death, and that is unrighteousness. So I will not adopt the attitude of avoiding disasters.

【注释】

苟：随便。辟：同"避"。

【译文】

孟子说："生命虽然是我所宝贵的，但对我来说还有比生命更为宝贵的，那就是义。所以我不做苟且偷生的事。死亡是我所厌恶的，但还有比死亡更为我所厌恶的，那就是不义。所以我不做贪生怕死的事。"

声闻过情，君子耻之

A gentleman is ashamed of his reputation surpassing his qualities.

声闻过情，君子耻之。

《孟子·离娄下》

A gentleman is ashamed of his reputation surpassing his qualities.

【注释】

声闻：名声，名誉。孟子弟子徐辟说："孔子曾数次称赞水，说'水呀，水呀！'他到底称赞水什么呢？"孟子说："有源之水汩汩而流，昼夜不停，漫过坎地，奔流向前，一直注入海洋。孔子就是赞扬水之有源这一点。假如是无源之水，一到雨季就沟渠盈满，但很快就干涸了。"孟子以无源之水喻名不副实。

【译文】

孟子说："君子以名不副实为耻。"

士窮不失義

Scholars will not drop righteousness in adversity...

老人家说系列丛书

士穷不失义，达不离道。

《孟子·尽心上》

Scholars will not drop righteousness in adversity, nor will they diverge from their principles in times of success.

【注释】

穷：困厄，穷困。达：显贵。道：引申为政治路线。《论语·学而》："礼之用，和为贵，先王之道，斯为美，小大由之。"

【译文】

孟子说："读书人困厄时不失义，显贵时不离道。"

顺天者存，逆天者亡

Those who follow Heaven's will survive and those who disobey Heaven's will perish.

顺天者存，逆天者亡。

《孟子·离娄上》

Those who follow Heaven's will survive and those who disobey Heaven's will perish.

【注释】

孟子认为："国家政治清明，道德低的人听命于道德高的人，一般人听命于贤人。国家政治黑暗，力量大的奴役力量小的，强的奴役弱的。这两种情况都是由天命决定的。"

【译文】

孟子说："天命是不可违的。顺从天命者生存，违背天命者灭亡。"

虽有天下易生之物也

Even a plant that grows readily will not be able to grow...

虽有天下易生之物也，一日暴之，十日寒之，未有能生者也。

《孟子·告子上》

Even a plant that grows readily will not be able to grow if it is exposed to the sun for one day and to the bitter cold for ten days.

【注释】

一日暴之，十日寒之：暴同"曝"，晒。成语"一暴十寒"源于此。

【译文】

孟子说："就是一种最易成活的植物，如果对它晒一天，冻十天，它也是长不好的。"

天将降大任于是人也

When Heaven intends to bestow a great mission on a person. . .

天将降大任于是人也，必先苦其心志，劳其筋骨，饿其体肤，空乏其身，行拂乱其所为，所以动心忍性，曾益其所不能。

《孟子·告子下》

When Heaven intends to bestow a great mission on a person, it makes him suffer in mind and body. It makes him endure starvation, and subjects him to poverty, difficulties and all kinds of tests so as to harden his will power, toughen his nature and increase his capabilities.

【注释】

心志：心意，志向。忍性：坚忍其性。曾：同"增"。所不能：原来没有的，不会的知识（技能）。

【译文】

孟子说："天将要把重大使命赋予某人时，必先苦其心志，劳其筋骨，饿其体肤，使他穷困让他历经磨炼，这样，便可以坚强他的心，坚韧他的性情，增长他的能力。"

天时不如地利

Favorable weather is less important than advantageous terrain.

天时不如地利，地利不如人和。

《孟子·公孙丑下》

Favorable weather is less important than advantageous terrain, and advantageous terrain is less important than unity among the people.

【注释】

天时、地利、人和：天时、地利、人和是当时成语，而其内容时有所变。孟子在这里讲的天时是指阴晴寒暑之是否与攻战有利。地利则指高城深池、山川险阻。人和则指人心所向。

【译文】

孟子说："在战争中，天时不及地利重要，地利不及人和重要。"

天下不心服而王者，未之有也

One can never unify the world if the hearts of all the people are not won over.

从来没有天下人心
不服而能统一天下的。

天下不心服而王者，未之有也。

《孟子·离娄下》

One can never unify the world if the hearts of all the people are not won over.

【注释】

天下不心服而王者：孟子的意思是：如果用仁义礼智使人屈服是办不到的，如果用仁义礼智去教育人，却能使人心服，只有使天下人心服才能统一天下，从来没有天下人心不服而能统一天下的。

【译文】

孟子说："从来没有天下人心不服而能统一天下的。"

天下溺，援之以道

If all the people of the world are drowning, they are to be saved by means of the Way.

天下溺，援之以道；嫂溺，援之以手——子欲手援天下乎？

《孟子·离娄上》

If all the people of the world are drowning, they are to be saved by means of the Way. A drowning sister-in-law is to be saved with the hand. Do you expect me to save all the people in the world with my hand?

【注释】

天下溺，援之以道：孟子决定离开齐国，齐王派淳于髡去挽留孟子，淳于髡问："男女之间，授受不亲，这是礼制吗？"孟子回答说："是礼制。"淳于髡说："那么，假如眼看着嫂嫂掉到水里，可以用手去拉她吗？"孟子说："看见嫂嫂掉到水里，不去拉她，这简直是豺狼。男女之间授受不亲，这是常礼。看见嫂嫂掉到水里，用手去救她，这是变通的办法。"淳于髡说："现在天下人都掉在了水里，您不去救援，又是什么缘故呢？"孟子说了上面的话。

【译文】

孟子说："天下人都掉在水里了，要用'道'去援救；嫂嫂掉在水里，用手去援救——你难道要我用一双手去援救天下人吗？"

天下有道，小德役大德

When the world is in good order, people of low morality listen to people of high morality...

天下有道，小德役大德，小贤役大贤；天下无道，小役大，弱役强。

《孟子·离娄上》

When the world is in good order, people of low morality listen to people of high morality, and ordinary people listen to persons of virtue. When the world is in chaos, the powerful enslave the powerless, the strong enslave the weak.

【注释】

小德役大德：意谓"小德役于大德""于"字省略。

【译文】

孟子说："国家政治清明，道德低的人听命于道德高的人，一般人听命于贤人。国家政治黑暗，力量大的奴役力量小的，强的奴役弱的。"

天下有道，以道殉身

When the rule of the empire is in order, a gentleman immerses himself in principles.

天下有道，以道殉身；天下无道，以身殉道。

《孟子·尽心上》

When the rule of the empire is in order, a gentleman immerses himself in principles. When the rule of the state is in disorder, a gentleman will not spare his own life to practice principles.

【注释】

以道殉身："道"为"身"（己）所运用。意谓天下政治清明，"道"因之得以施行。**以身殉道**："身"（己）为"道"而牺牲。意谓天下政治黑暗，君子不惜为道而献身。

【译文】

孟子说："天下政治清明，道因之得以施行；天下政治黑暗，君子不惜为道的施行而献身。"

天下之本在国

Kingdoms are the basis of the empire...

天下之本在国，国之本在家，家之本在身。

《孟子·离娄上》

Kingdoms are the basis of the empire, families are the basis of a kingdom and individuals are the basis of a family.

【注释】

天下国家：孟子所说天下即指中国，国即指中国境内的各诸侯国。故儒家认为"身修而后家齐，家齐而后国治，国治而后天下平。"（《礼记·大学》）本：事物的根基和主体。

【译文】

孟子说："天下的基础是国，国的基础是家，家的基础是人。"

天下之言性也，则故而已矣

When one talks about the nature of something, he needs
to know how it comes to be what it is...

天下之言性也，则故而已矣。故者以利为本。

《孟子·离娄上》

When one talks about the nature of something, he needs to know how it comes to be what it is, and the key to knowing this is to see how it functions.

【注释】

性：本性。利：顺。

【译文】

孟子说："天下人论本性，只要能知道其所以然就行了。推求其所以然的基础是顺其自然之理。"

为高必因丘陵

Lofty platforms should be built on mountains.

为高必因丘陵，为下必因川泽；
为政不因先王之道，可谓智乎？

《孟子·离娄上》

Lofty platforms should be built on mountains；deep ponds should be dug in marshes. Would it be wise to run a state without following the ways of the ancient sages？

【注释】

因：依靠，根据。**先王之道**：圣王之道。儒家特指古代圣王尧、舜、禹，文、武、周公及商汤的治国之道，其根本内容是礼乐制度和仁义道德。

【译文】

孟子说："筑高台要凭借山陵，挖深池要凑沼泽之地。如果治理国家不凭借前代圣王之道，那能说是聪明吗？"

我善养吾浩然之气

I am good at cultivating the great moral force.

我善养吾浩然之气。

《孟子·公孙丑上》

I am good at cultivating the great moral force.

【注释】

浩然之气：正大刚直之气。也省称浩然。那么什么叫浩然之气呢？孟子说："这很难一下子讲清楚。这种气至大至刚。用正义去培养它，不能稍有伤害，这种气就会存在于天地之间，无所不在。这种气还必须和义与道相配合，否则就没有什么力量了。这种气是由正义的长期积累所产生的，不是一朝一夕所能取得的。只要做一件于心有愧的事，这种气就空了。"

【译文】

孟子说："我善于培养我的浩然之气。"

无恒产而有恒心者

Only scholars can be morally confident though they possess no property.

无恒产而有恒心者，惟士为能。

《孟子·梁惠王上》

Only scholars can be morally confident though they possess no property.

【注释】

恒产：指土地、田园、房屋等不动产。孟子认为一般老百姓如果没有恒产，就不会有坚定的道德观念。就会胡作非为，违法乱纪，什么事都干得出来。所以孟子要求执政者要使老百姓的产业收入上可以赡养父母，下足以抚养妻子儿女。好年成可以丰衣足食，坏年成也不至于饿死。

【译文】

孟子说："没有恒产，而却有坚定的道德观念，只有读书人才能做到。"

无为其所不为

Do not do what you should not do...

无为其所不为，无欲其所不欲，如此而已矣。

《孟子·尽心上》

Do not do what you should not do, and do not desire what you should not desire. That is all.

【注释】

无为：儒家指以德政感化人民，不施行刑治。《论语·卫灵公》："无为而治者，其舜也与。夫何为哉，恭己正南面而已矣。" 欲：私欲，贪欲。

【译文】

孟子说："不干不应干的事，不要不应要的东西，这样就行了。"

西子蒙不洁，则人皆掩鼻而过之

If Xi Zi were covered in filth，everyone would pass her by holding his nose.

西子蒙不洁，则人皆掩鼻而过之；虽有恶人，齐戒沐浴，则可以祀上帝。

《孟子·离娄下》

If Xi Zi were covered in filth, everyone would pass her by holding his nose. If an ugly man fasts and bathes he may offer sacrifices to the Lord of Heaven.

【注释】

西子：古代美女西施。恶人：面貌丑陋的人。齐：同"斋"。

【译文】

孟子说："如果西施满身肮脏，别人也会掩鼻而过；纵是面貌丑陋的人，如果斋戒沐浴，也可以祭祀上帝。"

贤者以其昭昭使人昭昭

Virtuous men, in instructing others, get themselves enlightened first...

贤者以其昭昭使人昭昭，今以其昏昏使人昭昭。

《孟子·尽心下》

Virtuous men, in instructing others, get themselves enlightened first, and then try to enlighten others with their enlightenment. But nowadays those who try to enlighten others are unenlightened themselves.

【注释】

昭昭：明白。昏昏：糊涂的样子。

【译文】

孟子说："贤者教导别人必先自己明白，然后才要求别人明白；今为人师者，自己还不明白，却用这些模模糊糊的东西要求别人明白。"

贤者在位，能者在职

Employ virtuous persons as officials and assign capable persons to important posts.

贤者在位，能者在职。

《孟子·公孙丑上》

Employ virtuous persons as officials and assign capable persons to important posts.

【注释】

贤者在位，能者在职：据朱熹等注解"贤者"和"能者"，"在位"和"在职"都有所区别。

【译文】

孟子说："使有德行和才能的人居于相当的官职。"

小固不可以敌大

It seems that a small kingdom cannot defeat a big kingdom.

小固不可以敌大，寡固不可以敌众，弱固不可以敌强。

《孟子·梁惠王上》

It seems that a small kingdom cannot defeat a big kingdom, a sparsely populated kingdom cannot defeat a densely populated kingdom, nor can a weak kingdom defeat a powerful kingdom.

【注释】

小固不可以敌大：这是孟子对齐宣王说的话，当时齐宣王欲效"齐桓、晋文"之事，孟子则劝他行仁政而统一天下，否则靠齐国的武力要征服天下的想法不过是"缘木求鱼"而已。

【译文】

孟子说："小国不可能征服大国，人口稀少的国家不可能征服人口众多的国家，弱国不可能征服强国。"

形色，天性也

Bodily form and appearance are endowed by Heaven. . .

形色，天性也；惟圣人然后可以践形。

《孟子·尽心上》

Bodily form and appearance are endowed by Heaven. Outer beauty must be enriched by inner beauty, but this can only be done by a sage.

【注释】

形色：外貌与容色。践形：体现人所天赋的品质。

【译文】

孟子说："人的身体容貌是天生的，这种外在的美要靠内在的美来充实它，只有圣人才能做到这一点。"

言近而指远者，善言也

Simple words with far-reaching meaning are good words.

言近而指远者，善言也；守约而施博者，善道也。

《孟子·尽心下》

Simple words with far-reaching meaning are good words. Principles easy to practice with good effects are good principles.

【注释】

言近：言语浅近，易于接受。指远：深远。守约：掌握要领，操持简单。施博：广大。

【译文】

孟子说："言语浅近，意义却深远的，是善言；操作简单，效果却广大的，是善道。"

言人之不善

What shall a man do when he meets with some misfortune. . .

言人之不善，当如后患何。

《孟子·离娄下》

What shall a man do when he meets with some misfortune in the future if he talks about others' shortcomings now?

【注释】

言人之不善：儒家主张责己严，待人宽。孔子主张"君子成人之美，不成人之恶"。（《论语·颜渊》）《大戴礼·曾子立事》："君子己善，亦乐人之善也。己能，亦乐人之能也。"

【译文】

孟子说："尽说别人的坏话，日后祸患来了，自己怎么办呢？"

言无实不祥

It is not right to utter empty words...

言无实不祥。不祥之实，蔽贤者当之。

《孟子·离娄下》

It is not right to utter empty words; empty words come from those who stifle criticism and suggestions.

【注释】

实：与"虚"相对。可理解为结果，内容。祥：好，吉利。蔽贤：蔽，遮挡。蔽贤，埋没贤才，堵塞贤路。《国语·齐语》："于子之乡，有拳勇股肱之力秀出于众者，有则以告。有而不以告，谓之蔽贤。"

【译文】

孟子说："言之无物是不好的，这是由堵塞贤路者造成的。"

养心莫善于寡欲

The best way to cultivate one's heart is to reduce one's desires.

养心莫善于寡欲。其为人也寡欲，虽有不存焉者，寡矣；其为人也多欲，虽有存焉者，寡矣。

《孟子·尽心下》

The best way to cultivate one's heart is to reduce one's desires. When one's desires are few, the merits that he loses will be few also. With numerous desires, one can hardly keep much goodness.

【注释】

养心：修养心性。寡欲：少欲，节制贪欲。不存、有存：指"善性"的丧失或保留。《孟子·离娄下》："人之所以异于禽兽者几希，庶民去之，君子存之。"《孟子·告子上》："虽存乎人者，岂无仁义之心哉?"

【译文】

孟子说："修养心性的方法最好是节制贪欲。一个人少贪欲，善性丧失就少；贪欲多，其善性就不多了。"

仰不愧于天

The second delight of a gentleman is that he feels no shame as he faces Heaven above. . .

仰不愧于天，俯不怍于人。

《孟子·尽心上》

The second delight of a gentleman is that he feels no shame as he faces Heaven above and the people here below.

【注释】

孟子说君子有三种快乐的事：一是父母健康，兄弟平安；二是上无愧于天，下无愧于人；三是得天下英才而教育之。**怍**：惭愧。

【译文】

孟子说："上无愧于天，下无愧于人，是人生最快乐的事。"

尧舜之道

Even with Yao and Shun's statecraft. . .

尧舜之道，不以仁政，不能平治天下。

《孟子·离娄上》

Even with Yao and Shun's statecraft, no one can dominate the world without policies of benevolence.

【注释】

尧舜：唐尧和虞舜，远古部落联盟的首领。古史相传为圣明之君，孔子"祖述尧舜，宪章文武"，（《礼记·中庸》）孟子"言必称尧舜"（《孟子·滕文公上》）都以尧舜并称。

【译文】

孟子说："即使有尧舜之道，如果不行仁政，也不能平治天下。"

一正君而国定矣

When rulers'errors are corrected their kingdoms will be stable.

一正君而国定矣。

《孟子·离娄上》

When rulers' errors are corrected their kingdoms will be stable.

【注释】

孟子说："君主仁，没有人不仁。君主义，没有人不义。君主正，没有人不正。"（《孟子·离娄上》）

【译文】

孟子说："只要君主端正了，国家就安定了。"

以力服人者，非心服也

When one dominates others by force, they do not submit to him sincerely...

以力服人者，非心服也，力不赡也；以德服人者，中心悦而诚服也。如七十子之服孔子也。

《孟子·公孙丑上》

When one dominates others by force, they do not submit to him sincerely, but do so because they are not powerful enough to resist. When one dominates others by morality, they submit gladly, as his 70 disciples respected Confucius.

【注释】

赡（shàn）：充足，丰富。"力不赡"即力不足也。七十子：孔子弟子中身通六艺者的通称。

【译文】

孟子说："以力服人者，人不会心服，只是因为人家没有对抗的实力；以道德服人者，人才会心悦诚服，好像孔子的七十多位弟子归服于他那样。"

以佚道使民，雖勞不怨

If people are employed in order to ease their lot, they will not begrudge it even if they are driven hard.

以佚道使民，虽劳不怨。以生道杀民，虽死不怨杀者。

《孟子·尽心上》

If people are employed in order to ease their lot, they will not begrudge it even if they are driven hard. If people are killed for the sake of saving others' lives, even those who are killed will not begrudge those who kill them.

【注释】

佚：安乐，通"逸"。生：活着，生活着。

【译文】

孟子说："为了老百姓的安乐而役使百姓，百姓虽劳苦而无怨。为了老百姓的生命安全而杀死坏人，被杀者也不会怨恨杀他的人。"

友也者，友其德也

When one befriends others, what he should take into consideration is the others' good qualities and not other things.

友也者，友其德也。

《孟子·万章下》

When one befriends others, what he should take into consideration is the others' good qualities and not other things.

【注释】

友其德：这是孟子关于交友及朋友之间交往的原则。孔子主张"以文会友，以友辅仁。"（《论语·颜渊》）孟子主张"友其德"即"不挟长、不挟贵、不挟兄弟而友。"（《孟子·万章下》）孟子认为朋友之间"责善，朋友之道也"。（《孟子·离娄下》）

【译文】

孟子说："交朋友，是看中朋友的品德而交。"

有不虞之譽

There is unexpected praise and highly demanding censure.

有不虞之誉，有求全之毁。

《孟子·离娄上》

There is unexpected praise and highly demanding censure.

【注释】

不虞：虞（yú），意料，料度。不虞，没有料到。**求全之毁**：求全，希求完美无缺。朱熹《孟子集注》："求免于毁而反致毁，是为求全之毁。"后谓一心想保全声誉，反而受到诋毁。

【译文】

孟子说："有意想不到的赞誉，也有过于苛求的诋毁。"

有恒产者有恒心

People observe moral concepts and codes of behavior only when they have regular incomes from their property.

有恒产者有恒心，无恒产者无恒心。

《孟子·滕文公上》

People observe moral concepts and codes of behavior only when they have regular incomes from their property. If they do not have regular incomes they disregard morality.

【注释】

有恒产者有恒心，无恒产者无恒心：恒产指土地、房屋、田园等不动产。恒心指持久不变的意志。孟子又说过"无恒产而有恒心者，惟士为能"的话。（《孟子·梁惠王上》）

【译文】

孟子说："有固定产业收入的人才可能有一定的道德观念和行为准则，没有固定产业收入的人就不会有一定的道德观念和行为准则。"

有为者辟若掘井

Trying to achieve something is like digging a well...

有为者辟若掘井，掘井九轫而不及泉，犹为弃井也。

《孟子·尽心上》

Trying to achieve something is like digging a well—even if it is dug down 60 or 70（Chinese）feet but fails to reach the spring, it is no better than an abandoned well.

【注释】

轫：同"仞"，古代七尺（一说八尺）为一仞。

【译文】

孟子说："做事就像挖井一样，尽管挖了六七丈深，不见泉水仍然是一口废井。"

鱼，我所欲也

Fish is what I want. . .

孟子说

鱼，我所欲也，熊掌亦我所欲也；二者不可得兼，舍鱼而取熊掌者也。生亦我所欲也，义亦我所欲也；二者不可得兼，舍生而取义者也。

《孟子·告子上》

Fish is what I want and bear's paw is also what I want. If I cannot have both, I prefer bear's paw to fish. Life is what I treasure and righteousness is also what I treasure. If I cannot have both, I prefer righteousness to life.

【注释】

得兼：兼得，同时得到。

【译文】

孟子说："鱼是我喜欢吃的，熊掌也是我喜欢吃的，如果两者不能同时得到，我便会舍鱼而取熊掌。生命是我所宝贵的，义也是我所宝贵的。如果两者发生矛盾，必须舍弃一种时，我便会牺牲生命，而取义。"

域民不以封疆之界

National border alone can not stop people from fleeing.

域民不以封疆之界，固国不以山
豀之险，威天下不以兵革之利。

《孟子·公孙丑下》

National border alone can not stop people from fleeing,
precipitous terrain alone can not insure the security of the
state, and force alone can not subjugate the world.

【注释】

域：界限。豀：山谷。

【译文】

孟子说:"单靠疆界不足以约束人民。单靠山川的险
阻不足以保护国家的安全。单靠武力不足以威震天下。"

欲贵者，人之同心也

Everyone shares the aspiration for honor.

欲贵者，人之同心也。人人有贵于己者，弗思耳矣。人之所贵者，非良贵也。

《孟子·告子上》

Everyone shares the aspiration for honor. Everyone has something honorable in himself he has never noticed. Honor bestowed by others is not true honor.

【注释】

弗：不，弗思，不去想。**良贵**：真正的尊贵。

【译文】

孟子说："希望尊贵，这是人们共有的心理。但每个人自身都有可尊贵的东西，只是不肯认真想它罢了。别人所给的尊贵，不是真正的尊贵。"

执中无权，犹执一也

To adhere to the middle way without being flexible is being stubbornly biased.

执中无权，犹执一也。所恶执一者，为其贼道也，举一而废百也。

《孟子·尽心上》

To adhere to the middle way without being flexible is being stubbornly biased. Why should I detest stubborn bias? Because it hurts the way of benevolence and righteousness. It sticks to one point without taking other points into account.

【注释】

执中：中庸之道，称作事无过无不及为执中。权：变通，机变。执一：固执不变。贼：伤害，损害，败坏。

【译文】

孟子说："主张中庸如果不知变通，便是偏执。为什么厌恶偏执呢？因为它损害仁义之道，只是执其一点而不顾其余。"

志士不忘在沟壑

A person with lofty ideals would not hesitate to have his corpse abandoned in the wilderness.

志士不忘在沟壑，勇士不忘丧其元。

《孟子·滕文公下》

A person with lofty ideals would not hesitate to have his corpse abandoned in the wilderness, and a courageous person would not spare his life to do what is right.

【注释】

志士：有远大志向的人。沟壑：山沟，坑。丧：失去。元：头，首。

【译文】

孟子说:"有志之士为坚守节操不怕弃尸荒野，勇敢的人见义而为不怕掉脑袋。"

中也养不中

Men of lofty morality should educate and influence men of doubtful morality.

中也养不中，才也养不才，故人乐有贤父兄也。

《孟子·离娄下》

Men of lofty morality should educate and influence men of doubtful morality; men of talent should educate and influence untalented men. For everyone delights in having a talented and highly moral superior.

【注释】

中也养不中，才也养不才：朱熹《孟子集注》："无过不及之谓中，足以有为之谓才；养，谓涵育薰陶，俟其自化也。"中，即中庸，儒家认为做人的标准。

【译文】

孟子说："道德高尚的人来教育影响道德不高的人，才能高的人来教育影响才能低下的人，所以每个人都希望有个才德高尚的长者。"

诸侯之宝三

For the lords of the states there are three treasures.

诸侯之宝三：土地，人民，政事。宝珠玉者，殃必及身。

《孟子·尽心下》

For the lords of the states there are three treasures: land, people and government. Those who value pearls and jade above these are sure to bring disaster on themselves.

【注释】

宝珠玉者：以珠玉为宝者。珠玉，珠和玉。《孟子·梁惠王下》："昔者大王居邠，狄人侵之，……事之以珠玉，不得免焉。"

【译文】

孟子说："诸侯有三宝：土地，百姓和政治。如果以珍珠美玉为宝，一定会祸及其身。"

尊贤使能

A king should respect virtuous persons, employ capable persons. . .

尊贤使能，俊杰在位。

《孟子·公孙丑上》

A king should respect virtuous persons, employ capable persons and put outstanding persons in posts so as to give full play to their wisdom and capabilities.

【注释】

贤能：贤良有才能之人。俊杰：朱熹《孟子集注》云："俊杰，才德之异于众者。"

【译文】

孟子说："尊重有道德的人，重用有才能的人，使杰出的人物都有发挥才干的机会。"

图书在版编目（CIP）数据

孟子说/蔡希勤编注.—北京：华语教学出版社， 2006
　（中国圣人文化丛书.老人家说系列）
ISBN 978-7-80200-212-8

Ⅰ.孟… Ⅱ.蔡… Ⅲ.汉语—对外汉语教学—语言读物　Ⅳ.H195.5

中国版本图书馆 CIP 数据核字（2006）第 071862 号

出版人：单　瑛

责任编辑：韩　晖　　封面设计：胡　湖
印刷监制：佟汉冬　绘　图：李士伋

老人家说·孟子说

蔡希勤　编注
*

© 华语教学出版社
华语教学出版社出版
（中国北京百万庄大街 24 号　邮政编码 100037）
电话：(86)10-68320585
传真：(86)10-68326333
网址：www.sinolingua.com.cn
电子信箱：hyjx@ sinolingua.com.cn
北京松源印刷有限公司印刷
中国国际图书贸易总公司海外发行
（中国北京车公庄西路 35 号）
北京邮政信箱第 399 号　邮政编码 100044
新华书店国内发行
2006 年（32 开）第一版
2007 年第一版第二次印刷
2009 年第一版第三次印刷
（汉英）
ISBN 978-7-80200-212-8
9-CE-3729P
定价：29.80 元